# Brain Aerobics

## Word Games and Puzzles to Reinforce Basic Language Arts Skills

**Author:** R.E. Myers
**Editor:** Mary Dieterich
**Proofreaders:** Cindy Neisen and Margaret Brown

COPYRIGHT © 2018 Mark Twain Media, Inc.

ISBN 978-1-62223-699-2

Printing No. CD-405022

Mark Twain Media, Inc., Publishers
Distributed by Carson-Dellosa Publishing LLC

The purchase of this book entitles the buyer to reproduce the student pages for classroom use only. Other permissions may be obtained by writing Mark Twain Media, Inc., Publishers.

*All rights reserved. Printed in the United States of America.*

**Visit us at www.carsondellosa.com**

# TABLE OF CONTENTS

| Page | Title | Lesson |
|---|---|---|
| 1 | Introduction | |
| 2 | Missing Something | *Forming Words by Adding "E" (Long and Short Vowels)* |
| 5 | The "I's" Have It! | *Transforming Words by Adding "I"* |
| 7 | It's Up to "U" | *Transforming Words by Adding "U"* |
| 9 | Gloryjumpers and Spoilworms | *Inventing Compound Words* |
| 11 | The Rhyming Game | *Matching Rhyming Phrases With Definitions* |
| 12 | The Rhyming Game #2 | *Matching Rhyming Phrases With Definitions* |
| 13 | Triangles | *Putting Words Into Triangles; Completing Sentences* |
| 14 | More Triangles | *Putting Words Into Triangles; Completing Sentences* |
| 16 | Three-Way Triangles | *Putting Words Into Triangles* |
| 18 | A License Plate Game | *Inventing Sentences Based on License Plates; Writing a Paragraph* |
| 20 | Another License Plate Game | *Inventing Sentences Based on License Plates; Writing a Short Story* |
| 22 | Find the Twisted Word | *Deciphering Words Embedded in a Matrix* |
| 23 | More Twisted and Hidden Words | *Deciphering Words Embedded in a Matrix* |
| 24 | Magic Squares | *Solving Magic Square Puzzles* |
| 26 | More (and Harder) Magic Squares | *Solving Magic Square Puzzles* |
| 28 | Mr. Reynolds' Maze | *Solving a Secret Code* |
| 29 | Jumbles | *Putting Words in Proper Order* |
| 32 | Can You Reverse Them? | *Making Sense of Reversed Sayings* |
| 34 | Fractured School Words | *Putting Together Broken-Up Words* |
| 35 | Fractured Sports Terms | *Putting Together Broken-Up Words* |
| 36 | Either Way | *Composing Palindromic Sentences* |
| 38 | A Palindromic Portrait | *Composing an Acrostic; Writing a Character Sketch* |
| 39 | Find the Word | *Finding Hidden Words in Grids* |
| 42 | Animals in Hiding | *Finding the Names of Animals in Words* |
| 44 | Answer Keys | |

# INTRODUCTION

Part of the conventional wisdom concerning motivating young people to learn is that they will acquire concepts and skills more readily if they are engaged in a game-like activity. Young people enjoy games of all sorts. The attractiveness of games was one of the principal notions that inspired the writing of this book. All of the activities contain games of one kind or another, and we hope to induce your students to learn when they engage in the games.

This book includes some new games and a few familiar ones with a new twist. Students will need to use their reasoning skills and creativity to solve the puzzles and complete the games. Many of the games are designed to reinforce a grammar principle or to highlight vocabulary words.

Some of the games are quite challenging, but others are easy enough for students of diverse abilities. By tackling part or all of an activity yourself, you can determine whether it is suitable for your class. Also, you should feel at liberty to alter the activities in any way you wish in order to make them appropriate for your students.

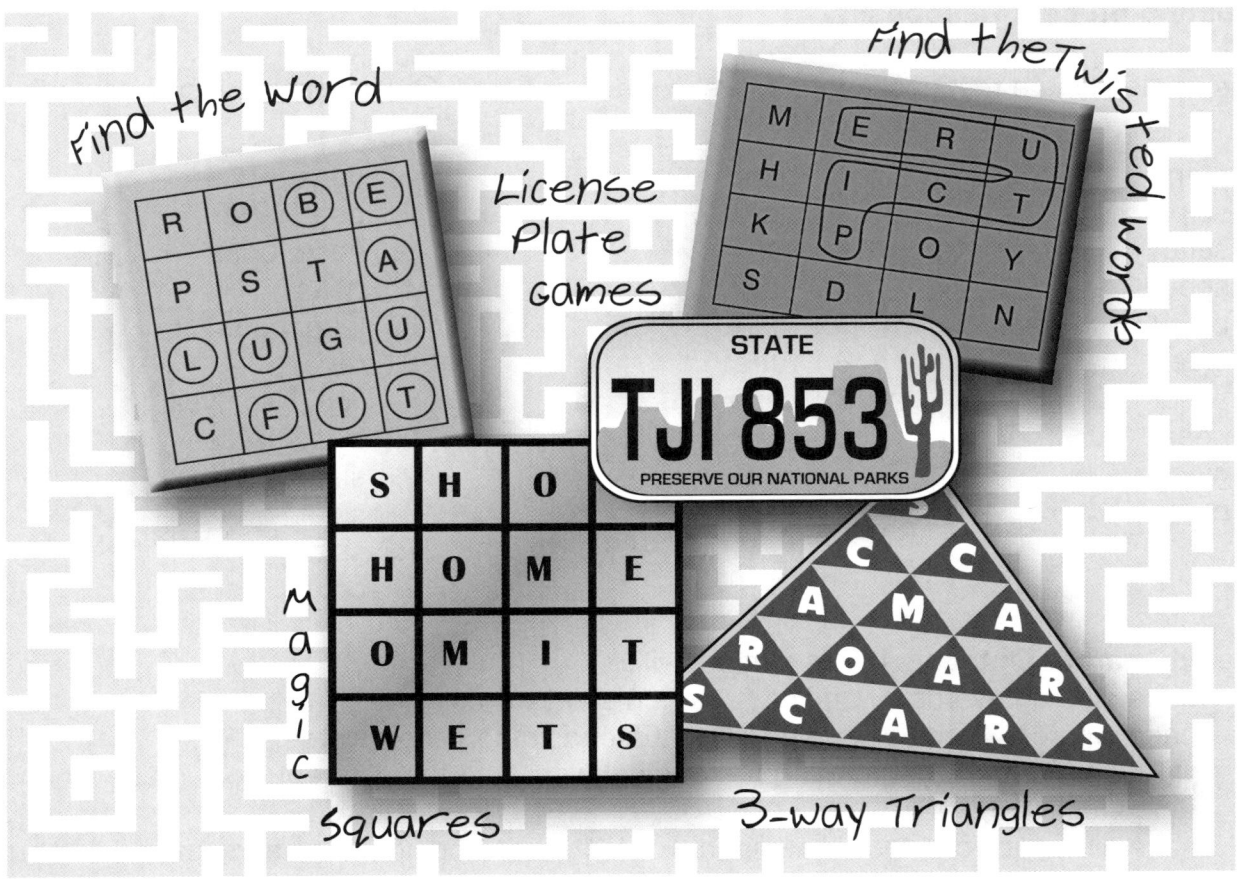

# MISSING SOMTHING

*Forming Different Words by Adding "E"*

## Teacher's Guide

**About the Lesson:**

"Missing Somthing" has three parts. The first part is a little word game in which the letter "e" is added to ten short words; the letters of the words remain in the same order. The second part has the student adding an "e" at the end of ten more short words, thus making different words in which the preceding vowels become long. Then the student makes up a sentence that includes one of the original words and the word it becomes after "e" is added. The last part of the lesson is the most challenging: the letters of 12 short words are to be rearranged to make different words when the letter "e" is added. A definition is required for each new word. Those students who are good at anagrams will race through most of the lesson, but many students will puzzle over quite a few of the prompts. The challenge for many students will come in defining words such as *lien, node, peat, spiel,* and *copes.* Students should be encouraged to use their dictionaries. They can add these words to their vocabularies.

**Evaluating Student Responses:**

These are legitimate responses to the three sets of prompts. Others may also be acceptable.

| A. | B. | C. |
|---|---|---|
| 1. prime | 1. hope | 1. done, node |
| 2. snipe | 2. pare | 2. peat, tape |
| 3. suite | 3. site | 3. nose, ones |
| 4. speed | 4. bare | 4. peas |
| 5. bleed | 5. mare | 5. leap, peal |
| 6. steep | 6. rube | 6. race |
| 7. fiend | 7. cape | 7. lien, Nile, Neil |
| 8. heard | 8. mate | 8. tread, trade |
| 9. niece | 9. cute | 9. sieve |
| 10. bread | 10. cope | 10. spiel |
| | | 11. spine |
| | | 12. copes, Pecos |

**Targeted Learner Outcomes:** The student will:
- make different words by adding "e" to ten short words.
- make different words by adding "e" to the ends of ten short words.
- write a sentence incorporating the original word and the different word made when "e" is added to its end.
- make different words out of 12 short words by rearranging their letters and adding an "e."
* define each of the 12 words that have been made.

Brain Aerobics  Missing Somthing

Name: _____ Date: _____

# MISSING SOMTHING

A. Is there something missing in the title of this lesson? Yes, it is the letter "e," of course. Add an "e" to the words below to form different words. For example, if the word given is *grip*, by adding an "e," you can make it *gripe*. If you aren't sure of the spelling of a word, check it out in the dictionary.

1. prim _____  2. snip _____

3. suit _____  4. sped _____

5. bled _____  6. step _____

7. find _____  8. hard _____

9. nice _____  10. brad _____

B. When you add an "e" to the end of most words in English, the preceding vowel is changed from a short sound to a long sound, as in the example above when *grip* becomes *gripe*. Add an "e" to the ends of the words below.

1. hop _____  2. par _____

3. sit _____  4. bar _____

5. mar _____  6. rub _____

7. cap _____  8. mat _____

9. cut _____  10. cop _____

Now make up a sentence using one of the word pairs above (both the word with the "e" and the original word without the "e").

_____

_____

_____

_____

Brain Aerobics                                                                                    Missing Somthing

Name: _____   Date: _____

## MISSING SOMTHING (cont.)

C.  Add an "e" to the words below and also rearrange their letters in order to form new words. For example, if you were given the word *lump*, by rearranging the letters and adding an "e," you could come up with *plume*. Define each of your new words. If you aren't sure of the meaning of a word, check it out in a dictionary.

1. nod _____  _____

2. pat _____  _____

3. son _____  _____

4. sap _____  _____

5. pal _____  _____

6. arc _____  _____

7. nil _____  _____

8. dart _____  _____

9. vies _____  _____

10. lips _____  _____

11. nips _____  _____

12. cops _____  _____

# THE "I's" HAVE IT

*Transforming Words by Adding an "I"*

## Teacher's Guide

**About the Lesson:**

This game is a variation of the familiar anagram. It only has one extra feature—a letter is added to the word after its letters are rearranged. A few of the solutions will be hard to come up with, so you should not allow your students to be too concerned if they can't think of an answer.

To correctly respond to the eight items at the end of the lesson, a student must be able to tell the difference between a proper noun and a common noun. A response of *Ami* for *Ma*, for instance, would perhaps be satisfying but not correct. The word must be a noun, not a verb or an adjective. Therefore, if the student were given *Goren*, the word *ignore* wouldn't work.

**Evaluating Student Responses:**

These are satisfactory responses for set A:

1. wide
2. bite
3. wail
4. pipe
5. into
6. toil
7. time, item, mite
8. ideal
9. weird
10. eider
11. basic
12. suite
13. train
14. posit
15. media
16. tirade
17. detail, tailed
18. domain
19. praise
20. soiled

These are satisfactory responses for set B:

1. mile
2. tribe
3. lairs, liars
4. drain
5. chair
6. aim
7. hernia
8. goiter

Brain Aerobics                                    The "I's" Have It

# THE "I's" HAVE IT

**A.** See if you can make another word out of each of the words below by rearranging the letters and adding an "i." For example, if the word were *nap*, you could make the word *pain* out of it by rearranging the letters and adding an "i."

1. wed _____          2. bet _____
3. law _____          4. pep _____
5. ton _____          6. lot _____
7. met _____          8. lead _____
9. drew _____         10. deer _____
11. scab _____        12. suet _____
13. rant _____        14. stop _____
15. dame _____        16. trade _____
17. dealt _____       18. nomad _____
19. reaps _____       20. doles _____

**B.** Now make common nouns out of the proper nouns below by adding an "i" and rearranging the letters of each word. Proper nouns are names of particular people, places, and events, and they begin with capital letters. Common nouns are all the other nouns, and they are not capitalized.

1. Lem _____          2. Bert _____
3. Lars _____          4. Rand _____
5. Arch _____          6. Ma _____
7. Ahern _____         8. Roget _____

# IT'S UP TO "U"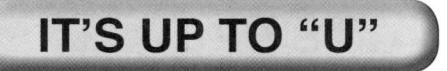

*Transforming Words by Adding a "U"*

## Teacher's Guide

**About the Lesson:**

Anagrams is a popular game with people young and old. "It's Up to 'U'" is such a game, except that it features a little grammar. The activity should be engaged in as a game, and you can administer it in that spirit.

<u>First Level: Making New Words Out of 20 Words by Adding a "U"</u>

At the first level of involvement, your students are to rearrange the letters of 20 words and add a "u" to each of them in order to form new words. Once they get the hang of it, the students won't be long in coming up with the words. It there are students who don't catch on right away, you might give another example to go with ours. The easiest one we can think of is *boy*, which becomes *buoy* with the addition of a "u."

<u>Second Level: Making Common Nouns and Verbs by Adding a "U" to Proper Nouns</u>

With some manipulation and patience, the common and proper nouns given can be converted to proper nouns or verbs by adding a "u." An example is *lap*, which becomes *Paul* with the "u" added. (Proper names are allowed in this part of the activity.)

**Evaluating Student Responses:**

These are answers to the prompts in the first part of the activity, although they are not the only answers possible:

A.
1. mute
2. aunt, tuna
3. daub
4. fuel
5. tune
6. nude, dune
7. gout
8. upset
9. usage
10. suede
11. cause
12. endue
13. super, purse
14. rogue, rouge
15. caulk
16. spouse
17. auger, argue
18. louver
19. sprout
20. grouse

B. These proper nouns can be made from the common nouns.
1. Paul   2. Bauer   3. Arum

These verbs can be made from the proper nouns.
4. urge   5. argue   6. rouse

7. The letter "u" often forms a diphthong with another vowel.

**Following Through:**

Check to see whether your students have produced words in the second section that are truly proper nouns or verbs.

# IT'S UP TO "U"

A. Here is a chance to show how you can make words change by rearranging their letters. Make more common nouns out of the common nouns below by adding a "u" to each word and rearranging the letters. For example, if the word *nod* were given and a "u" is added, you could make a new word, *undo*.

1. met _____
2. tan _____
3. bad _____
4. elf _____
5. ten _____
6. end _____
7. tog _____
8. step _____
9. ages _____
10. seed _____
11. case _____
12. need _____
13. reps _____
14. gore _____
15. lack _____
16. poses _____
17. gear _____
18. lover _____
19. strop _____
20. gorse _____

B. Make proper nouns out of these common nouns by adding a "u" and rearranging the letters.

1. lap _____
2. bear _____
3. arm _____

Now make verbs out of these proper nouns.

4. Reg _____
5. Gare _____
6. Rose _____

7. What have you noticed about the way "u" combines with other letters?

_____

_____

# GLORYJUMPERS AND SPOILWORMS

A compound word is a word formed by joining two or more words together. In the way our language naturally evolves, two separate words when used frequently together may be joined by a hyphen, and then they are later linked together permanently as one word. The meaning is the same for all three forms. For example, *tax payers, tax-payers,* and *taxpayers* in any case means "people who pay taxes."

Following are a dozen compound words that have never entered the English language. They were created by joining the different parts of twelve common compound words. Your task is to take each word part of the compound words and put the parts back together as they are supposed to be. Words may be placed on the lines below in any order.

1. spoilworm
2. doombug
3. gutterbrain
4. nitrat
5. scattersnipe
6. booksport
7. jittersayer
8. puddlehound
9. gladmouth
10. rugpicker
11. blabberhander
12. gloryjumper

1. _____
2. _____
3. _____
4. _____
5. _____
6. _____
7. _____
8. _____
9. _____
10. _____
11. _____
12. _____

# GLORYJUMPERS AND SPOILWORMS (cont.)

Now make up six more compound words from the 12 original words you have put together. After each of your new compound words, make up a definition. For example, *gloryjumpers* could be people who parachute from airplanes to gain fame. *Spoilworms* could very well be weevils.

1. _____
   _____

2. _____
   _____

3. _____
   _____

4. _____
   _____

5. _____
   _____

6. _____
   _____

Brain Aerobics

The Rhyming Game

Name: _____ Date: _____

# THE RHYMING GAME

*Willy-nilly, mumbo-jumbo, hanky-panky, helter-skelter*—we have a number of these rhyming pairs in our language. There are also *razzle-dazzle, namby-pamby, fuddy-duddy, harum-scarum, hurly-burly, roly-poly, lovey-dovey, hotsy-totsy, hoity-toity,* and *hurdy-gurdy*. We also have other expressions such as *fat cat, big wig, handy Andy, silly Billy,* and *culture vulture*.

A popular game based on rhyming pairs is called "hink-pink" or "hinky-pinky," depending upon whether the words have one or two syllables. You try to match two words with two rhyming words that mean the same.

Let's play the game with only one syllable for each of the paired words. For example, if you see *obese feline*, you can respond with *fat cat*. Try to find rhyming pairs for the words below. If you can't think of a synonym, use a dictionary or thesaurus to find a suitable word.

1. torrid child _____
2. sad friend _____
3. large hog _____
4. wonderful spouse _____
5. bashful lad _____
6. disgusting fashion _____
7. intelligent beginning _____
8. unusual twosome _____
9. strong material _____
10. superior police officer _____
11. phony reptile _____
12. bruin's den _____
13. recipe collection _____
14. dilatory enemy _____

See if you can think of six or more pairs of rhyming words. For each pair, give a definition in two or three words. Then write the definitions on another piece of paper. Challenge your classmates to come up with the rhyming pairs that match your definitions. You don't have to make all of the rhyming pairs one-syllable words; some pairs can be two syllables for each word.

**Rhymed pair**                                    **Definition**

_____    _____

_____    _____

_____    _____

_____    _____

_____    _____

# THE RHYMING GAME #2

Trying to think of a pair of rhyming words to match a definition is a popular game for people of all ages. The game is called "hink-pink" or "hinky-pinky," depending upon whether the rhymed pairs have one or two syllables each. If the words are supposed to have three syllables, it is called "hinkety-pinkety."

Let's play the game that has two syllables for each of the rhymed words. For example, if you are given *attractive cat,* you can respond with *pretty kitty.*

1. amusing rabbit _____
2. wounded hen _____
3. swollen-faced ruffian _____
4. cowardly man _____
5. clever Andrew _____
6. peculiar cash _____
7. slim seller _____
8. intelligent Theodore _____
9. wild act _____
10. heavy portsider _____
11. quite shaggy _____
12. famished Marv _____

See if you can come up with several hinky-pinkies. Write the rhymed words with their definitions, and then give the definitions to a classmate. Your classmate can also give you his or her definitions to match with rhymed words.

**Rhymed pair**                        **Definition**

_____

_____

_____

_____

_____

_____

# TRIANGLES

Below there are triangles with blank spaces. To the left of each triangle are four clues to help you fill in the blank spaces in each row of the triangle. The words you form will complete the sentences under the triangles.

1.
   a mild interjection

   the sign of the infinitive

   to gain a prize

   one time

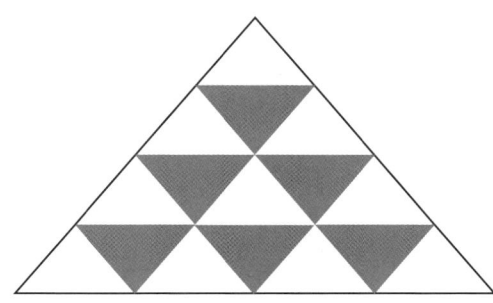

"___ ___ ___ ___ ___ ___ ___ ___ ___ ___!" Sheila exclaimed when she bought her lottery ticket.

2.
   first person singular (nominative case)

   giving emphasis to a verb

   like, appreciate (slang); use a shovel

   young males

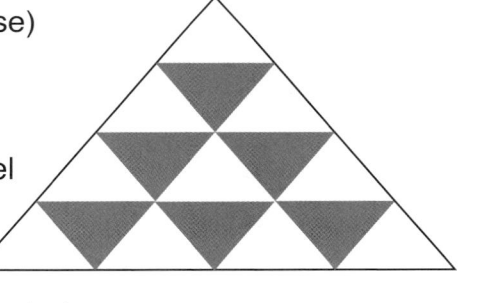

Little Karen said, "Some girls may not care for them, but ___ ___ ___ ___ ___ ___ ___ ___ ___ ___."

3.
   first person singular (nominative case)

   verb to be (present tense)

   more than enough

   chilled

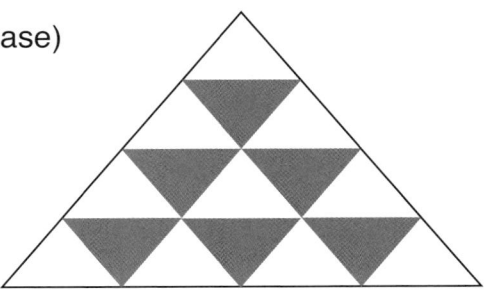

When asked why she didn't get in the water, Kaitlin answered: "___ ___ ___ ___ ___ ___ ___ ___ ___ ___!"

# MORE TRIANGLES

Below there are triangles with blank spaces. To the left of each triangle are four clues to help you fill in the blank spaces in each row of the triangle. The words you form will complete the sentences under the triangles.

1. 
   exclamation expressing surprise or wishfulness

   first person singular possessive pronoun

   opposite of good

   the top part of the body

   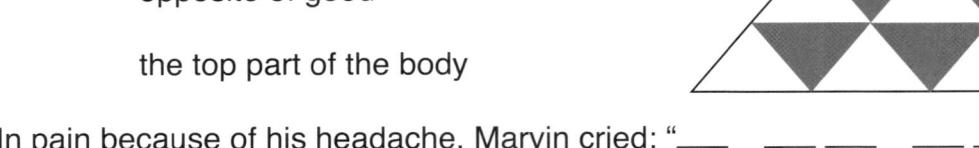

   In pain because of his headache, Marvin cried: "__  __ __  __ __ __  __ __ __ __!"

2. 
   an article (part of speech)

   negative

   past tense of *is*

   all right

   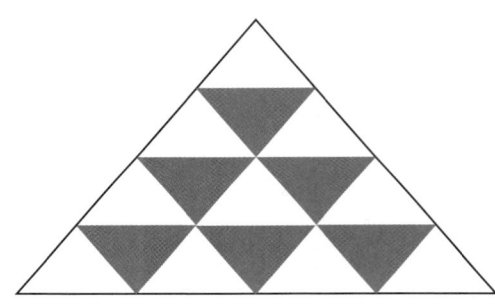

   When asked if they'd like to take the test right now, Mr. Martin assured his students that

   "__  '__ __'  __ __ __  __ __ __ __."

3. 
   exclamation expressing surprise or wishfulness

   the infinitive

   to strike

   with force

   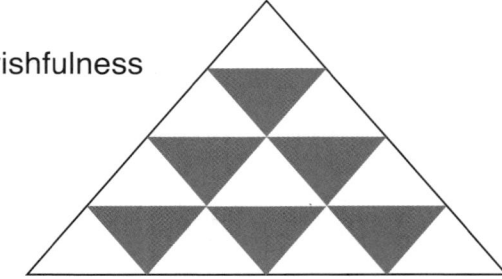

   Thinking about his weak batting, Paul muttered to himself, "__  __ __  __ __ __ __  __ __ __ __!"

# MORE TRIANGLES (cont.)

4.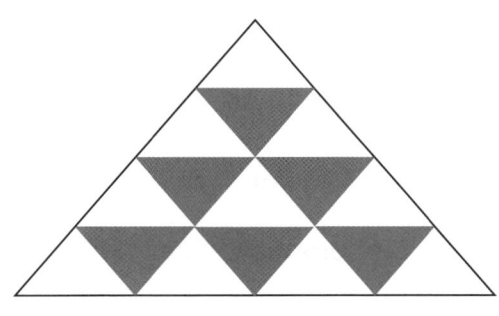

    first person singular (nominative case)

    verb to be (present tense)

    negative

    at this place

    While playing hide-and-seek, Mary told her brother to pretend like "___  ___ ___

    ___ ___ ___   ___ ___ ___ ___."

5.  See if you can provide clues for words in the blank spaces of the triangle below. Compose the beginning of a sentence that makes sense when the four words are added.

    Clues:

    _____

    _____

    _____

    _____

    Sentence:

    _____

    _____

    _____

# THREE-WAY TRIANGLES

Fill in the blank triangles by using the clues at the left. When you have finished, the three sides of the triangles should all spell the same word.

This is an example of how the game works:

the 19th letter of the alphabet

carbon copy; chief clerk

initials of the American Medical Association

a loud, deep rumbling sound

marks left on the skin after a wound

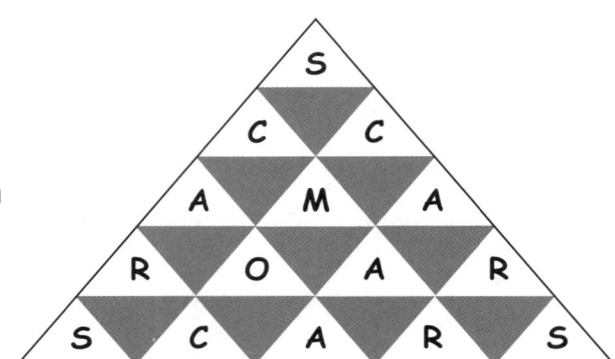

1. See if you can get the three sides of this triangle to say the same thing.

    an article (part of speech)

    a brand of candy

    Adam's wife

    an explosive

    a microbe (alternate spelling)

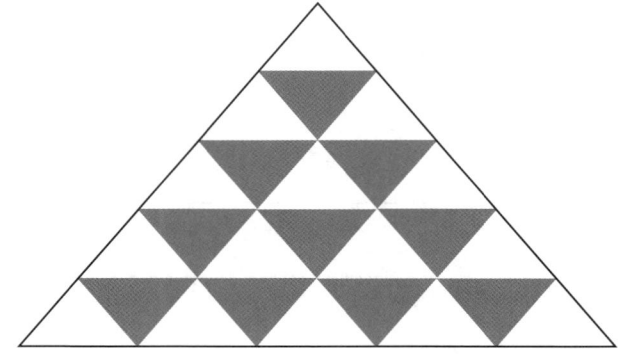

2. Here is another one for you to figure out.

    the 19th letter of the alphabet

    abbreviation for electrical engineer

    exclamation expressing satisfaction

    a portable shelter

    places or spaces to sit

# THREE-WAY TRIANGLES (cont.)

3. Finally, this is a bigger triangle with the same word on all three sides.

   the 18th letter of the alphabet

   initials of a famous American poet

   a feminine name

   an act; a document under seal

   to avoid

   one who interprets reading

4. See if you can devise a triangle like the ones above whose sides all spell the same word.

   Definitions:

   _____

   _____

   _____

   _____

Brain Aerobics                                                                                   A License Plate Game

# A LICENSE PLATE GAME

*Composing Sentences to Fit License Plates*

## Teacher's Guide

**About the Lesson:**

The license plate game can be quite challenging for some individuals. Nevertheless, with practice and a little loosening up of the brain's right hemisphere, it can be a lot of fun. Unlike vanity plates, regular license plate numbers are issued without preconceived ideas. (Occasionally there is one that makes a little sense, but this doesn't happen very often.) Like other games dealing with license plates, this one requires the players to be alert.

**Evaluating Student Responses:**

If your students are able to make up sentences for the dozen numbers in the lesson in less than 15 minutes, they will be doing well. No time limits should be imposed, however, and you should encourage all of your students to produce all 12 sentences. Have your students check to see that all of their sentences have a subject and a predicate.

These are the responses that came to my mind, but your students will get entirely different ideas. These sentences are offered only as examples. The evaluating should be in terms of whether the sentences have subjects and predicates.

| Plate | Sentence |
|---|---|
| SPM 045 | Simon Paul Morgan is 45. |
| 5 FPV 031 | Five friendly Polish visitors made 31 phone calls. |
| 615 PWM | Six hundred and fifteen pretty women married too soon. |
| 1 NBN 016 | One newborn nephew weighed 16 pounds. |
| DLK 111 | Dentists learning karate number 111. |
| 3 CS 3418 | Three crafty seamen sailed 3,418 miles in a dingy. |
| ICC 249 | Itinerant coaches cost less than 249 dollars per game. |
| 4UBT540 | Four utterly bald tires won't take you 540 more miles. |
| LEM 911 | Lamed elderly men can call 911. |
| 064 ARF | Sixty-four addled retirees fasted on Thanksgiving. |
| 3GQU296 | Three green quilts used 296 patches. |
| 1 VAD 201 | One very alert driver ignored 201 distractions. |

**Targeted Learner Outcomes:** The student will:
- compose sentences inspired by 12 license plates.
- make them complete sentences.

# A LICENSE PLATE GAME

Many young people get bored when making long trips in a car. To relieve their boredom and keep them occupied, a variety of games have been invented. One interesting game is called the license plate game. If you are riding along in a car and either pass a car or are passed by a car, you can read its license plate number. For instance, let's say that you spot a brown SUV with the license plate number TJI 853. You can make up a sentence that is based on those letters and numbers. It could be "Tearful Jane Ingle's badge number at Elmer's Onion Works is 853." ("She's the chief slicer," you say to yourself.) Sometimes the license plate won't inspire you, but the next time you see a license plate, see if you can make a sentence out of the number.

Can you make sentences out of these license plate numbers? Remember: a sentence has a subject and a predicate, and it has punctuation at the end.

SPM 045 _____

5 FPV 031 _____

615 PWM _____

1 NBN 016 _____

DLK 111 _____

3 CS 3418 _____

ICC 249 _____

4UBT540 _____

LEM 911 _____

064 ARF _____

3GQU296 _____

1 VAD 201 _____

Brain Aerobics — Another License Plate Game

# ANOTHER LICENSE PLATE GAME

Quite a number of people like to customize their license plates by requesting that their state put certain letters and numbers on their plates. We call these "vanity plates," and they are found throughout the country. Of course, these people who want to show their cleverness, occupation, or philosophy have to pay extra for their plates. It seems to satisfy both the states, which can always use more money, and the car owners, who want to show off a little. For example, a dentist has plates that tell the world he is a 2THDOC.

Below are some vanity plates that have been seen on the highways. Take a close look at each and then make some guesses about what the owners of these cars are like. A description of the car is given in parentheses. Jot down your guesses beneath each license plate. You might consider these matters when you imagine what an owner would be like:

- male or female
- preference in clothing
- hobbies
- age
- physical characteristics
- occupation
- personality

1. **4MAGIC** (Mercedes C230, green)

2. **STORK** (BMW 740i, silver)

3. **POSIES** (Chevrolet panel truck, red)

4. **TRYGOD** (Toyota Celica, white)

Brain Aerobics — Another License Plate Game

# ANOTHER LICENSE PLATE GAME (cont.)

5. DARKBRD   (Pontiac Trans Am, black)

_____

_____


6. UBFRE   (old Volkswagen van, orange)

_____

_____

_____


7. STAMPIN   (Cadillac Escalade SUB, black)

_____

_____

_____


8. TRIM   (Honda Accord, bright red)

_____

_____

_____

   Look over your notes about the eight car owners, and select one who especially interests you. Make that person the central character in a short story. The story needn't be about cars, however; it can be about anything in which the personality of the car owner determines the story's action and outcome.

   Your story should have all of the elements of a longer story—that is, characters, setting, and plot—and:
- an intriguing title,
- a beginning that interests the reader enough to keep on reading,
- a focus on a single incident or crisis, and
- enough action to hold the reader's attention.

Write the story on your own paper.

Brain Aerobics — Find the Twisted Word

# FIND THE TWISTED WORD

Find the seven-letter words hidden in these grids. Letters must touch. They run horizontally, vertically, backward, and forward, but not diagonally. It helps to circle the letters that go together.

Here is an example:

| M | E | R | U |
|---|---|---|---|
| H | I | C | T |
| K | P | O | Y |
| S | D | L | N |

The word is PICTURE.

1.

| Y | C | O | T |
|---|---|---|---|
| R | E | X | U |
| F | H | P | L |
| S | N | I | A |

The word is EXPLAIN.

2.

| R | Q | U | Y |
|---|---|---|---|
| E | A | Z | C |
| P | D | I | N |
| S | H | O | G |

The word is READING.

3.

| T | C | A | D |
|---|---|---|---|
| L | E | J | Y |
| I | W | O | R |
| N | U | S | P |

The word is PROJECT.

4.

| L | H | D | O |
|---|---|---|---|
| G | I | F | Z |
| U | M | Y | B |
| R | E | S | A |

The word is FIGURES.

Brain Aerobics                                                                                                       More Twisted and Hidden Words

Name: _____  Date: _____

# MORE TWISTED AND HIDDEN WORDS

Each grid below contains a seven-letter word. All of the letters in the word touch, but they don't go diagonally. Circle the letters and then write the word to the right of the grid. All the seven-letter words hidden in the grids have to do with language and writing.

Here is an example:

| U | Y | S | E |
|---|---|---|---|
| R | A | G | O |
| P | M | R | I |
| H | M | A | V |

The word is GRAMMAR.

1.

| P | S | I | T |
|---|---|---|---|
| K | A | P | A |
| Z | C | N | L |
| B | U | Y | O |

The word is _____.

2.

| R | O | Z | K |
|---|---|---|---|
| B | S | K | M |
| C | T | L | U |
| I | P | E | D |

The word is _____.

3.

| Y | L | O | P |
|---|---|---|---|
| E | W | S | G |
| A | R | I | N |
| M | U | T | I |

The word is _____.

4.

| A | S | E | P |
|---|---|---|---|
| N | I | R | K |
| F | O | Q | B |
| S | D | C | U |

The word is _____.

# MAGIC SQUARES

If you can determine what words are being defined at the left of the three matrixes below, you should be able to write four-letter words that can be read either across or down. This matrix is called a "magic square." Here is an example:

| | | | |
|---|---|---|---|
| S | H | O | W |
| H | O | M | E |
| O | M | I | T |
| W | E | T | S |

to indicate, demonstrate

a residence, abode

to leave out

moistens

Complete the following magic squares. If you get stuck, you can consult a dictionary or thesaurus.

1.
 to plead, advocate strongly

 a space in a building

 a desert plateau in eastern Asia

 to send out, give forth

2.
 a story or yarn

 eager and enthusiastic

 commercial spelling for reduced calories

 where Adam ate the apple

# MAGIC SQUARES (cont.)

3.

slang for photographs

a thought or scheme

a penny, one-hundredth of a dollar

to satisfy with more than enough

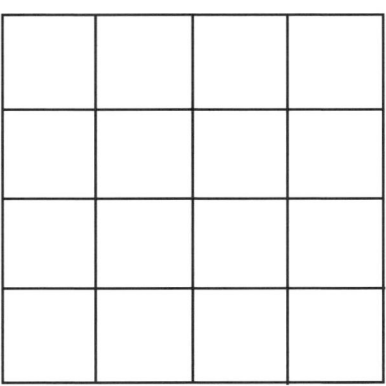

4. See if you can design a magic square. It is probably easier to solve one than it is to make one up, but give it your best shot. Write clues on the lines to match the words you want to fit in the magic square. When you are done, prepare a clean copy of the clues and a blank magic square on your own paper. Swap magic squares with a classmate, and try to solve each other's puzzles.

_____

_____

_____

_____

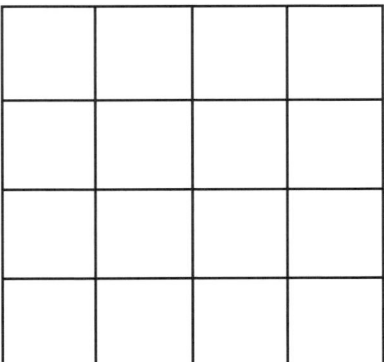

Brain Aerobics

Name: _____  Date: _____

# MORE (AND HARDER) MAGIC SQUARES

Magic squares can also be made up of five-letter words. See if you can solve the two magic squares below. Use a dictionary or thesaurus if you are stumped.

1.

to become aware; a faculty such as hearing or seeing

abnormal accumulation of fluid in the body

not ever

an odor; to use the olfactory sense

previous; opposite of late

2.

to talk

freedom from wars or quarrels

one who consumes food

sharp, biting, harsh in temper

British spelling for the concrete edges forming a gutter along a street

Brain Aerobics  
More (and Harder) Magic Squares

Name: _____ Date: _____

## MORE (AND HARDER) MAGIC SQUARES (cont.)

3. Five-letter magic squares may or may not be as easy to solve as four-letter squares, but they are definitely hard to make up. See if you can design one. When you are done, prepare a clean copy of the clues and a blank magic square in the space below. Cut the bottom section of this paper off, and swap magic squares with a classmate. Try to solve each other's puzzles.

_____

_____

_____

_____

_____

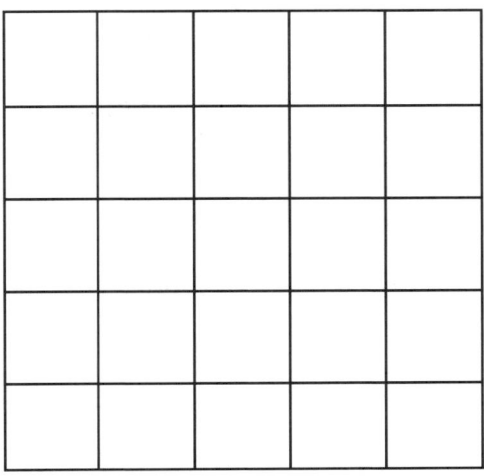

- - - - - - - - - - - - - - - - - - - - - - - - - - - - - - - - - - - - -

_____

_____

_____

_____

_____

CD-405022 ©Mark Twain Media, Inc., Publishers

Brain Aerobics  
Mr. Reynolds' Maze

Name: _____  Date: _____

# MR. REYNOLDS' MAZE

Walter thought he'd try the maze that Mr. Reynolds made in his cornfield. Although Walter had heard it was really difficult to get out of, he was confident that he would have no trouble. Mr. Reynolds had a simple plan for his maze. He wrote it out in code for his children, and they had no trouble getting through the maze because they had solved the code.

This is what Mr. Reynolds wrote:

YJGP  VJGTG  KU  C  EJQKEG  IQ  VQ  VJG  NGHV.

1. Solve the code and then trace your way through the maze. Hint: Look for recurring letters that could be vowels.

   What is the vowel that occurs most often in English words? _____

   What does Mr. Reynolds' message say? _____

   _____

**Exit**

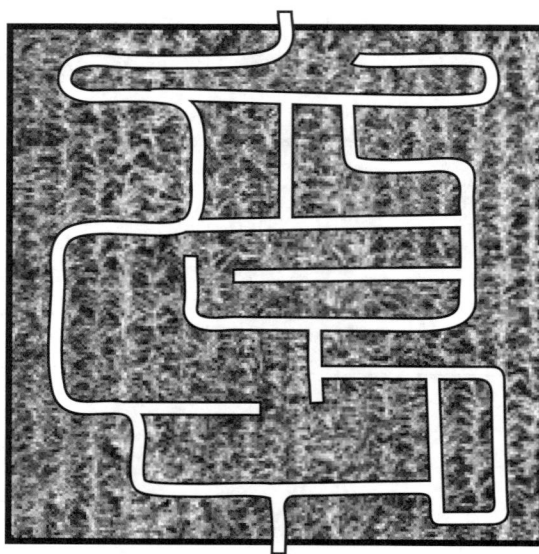

**Entrance**

2. It turned out not to be as easy as Walter thought the maze would be. If he could have sent out a message using Mr. Reynolds' code, it would have been:

   NGV  OG  QWV  QH  JGTG!

   What would Walter's message have said? _____

*Writing Sentences in the Proper Word Order*

## Teacher's Guide

**About the Lesson:**

The order in which English words are spoken comes naturally to native English speakers. We usually use the subject-verb-object order in clauses and sentences. We put adjectives before their nouns and, in general, put modifiers near the words that are modified. Accordingly, your students shouldn't have any difficulty in arranging the three columns of words into intelligible sentences. Some may have to make several stabs at organizing the words into sentences, but in all likelihood, the activity won't baffle your students.

**Evaluating Student Responses:**

These are acceptable ways to string the words together in writing the three sentences:

1. Pat went to the market with me and shopped for an hour.

   Pat went with me to the market and shopped for an hour.

2. Harry warily reached into the hole and grabbed the tiny creature.

   Harry reached into the hole and warily grabbed the tiny creature.

3. Ads called "spam" now get to us by means of the computer.

   Ads called "spam" get to us now by means of the computer.

   By means of the computer, ads called "spam" get to us now.

**Targeted Learner Outcomes:** The student will:

- think about conventional word order in English sentences.
- rearrange three columns of words into meaningful sentences.

# JUMBLES

In English we write from left to right. There are other languages where the writing and printing go from right to left. Some people have suggested that it would be easier if our eyes would drop down to the next line and then go from right to left. The pattern would be like the illustration below. However, it is extremely doubtful that we'll ever adopt such a system.

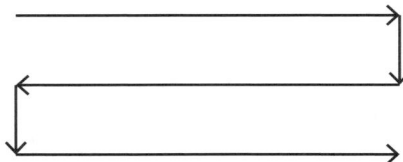

There is an accepted order in which our phrases and sentences are expressed. For instance, we don't say "girl pretty" or "the street into." In the following activity, there are three sentences that have been jumbled so that the words don't go in the conventional order.

Re-order the words so that you have three meaningful sentences. There may be more than one correct way to order the words in each of the sentences.

To illulstrate what you are to do, the following is a short sentence that was jumbled with the words stacked on top of one another.

**Example:** the
at
o'clock
right
time
arrived
three
mail
on

**Words in the correct order:**

The mail arrived right on time at three o'clock.

1. shopped
the
market
Pat
with
hour
went
to
and
for
an
me

# JUMBLES (cont.)

2. reached
   hole
   the
   and
   creature
   warily
   into
   the
   Harry
   tiny
   grabbed

3. now
   means
   computer
   us
   to
   "spam"
   get
   called
   the
   of
   by
   ads

Brain Aerobics

Can You Reverse Them?

Name: _____  Date: _____

## CAN YOU REVERSE THEM?

Have you heard the saying, "Haste makes waste"? If it is reversed, you have something that makes almost as much sense: "Waste makes haste." Often because we waste time, for instance, we have to hurry to catch up. Some sayings, then, can make sense when reversed.

Which of these sayings can be reversed and still make sense? You should be able to reverse at least five of them and get some meaning from them. Write the saying, the reversal, and an explanation of the new meaning on the blanks on the next page.

1. May all your troubles be small ones.

2. Where there's a will, there's a way.

3. Time waits for no one.

4. Nobody loves a loser.

5. It's better to be safe than sorry.

6. Don't count your chickens before they're hatched.

7. Beggars can't be choosers.

8. A penny saved is a penny earned.

9. The bigger they are, the harder they fall.

10. Still waters run deep.

11. He laughs best who laughs last.

12. If the shoe fits, wear it.

13. All that glitters isn't gold.

14. Many hands make light work.

Name: _____  Date: _____

## CAN YOU REVERSE THEM? (cont.)

1. Familiar saying: _____

   Reversal: _____

   Explanation: _____

2. Familiar saying: _____

   Reversal: _____

   Explanation: _____

3. Familiar saying: _____

   Reversal: _____

   Explanation: _____

4. Familiar saying: _____

   Reversal: _____

   Explanation: _____

5. Familiar saying: _____

   Reversal: _____

   Explanation: _____

6. Familiar saying: _____

   Reversal: _____

   Explanation: _____

# FRACTURED SCHOOL WORDS

There are 17 words commonly heard in school that have been broken up into two or three parts in the matrix below. Using each part only once, put the word parts together and write the school words on the blanks below.

| du | mar | tory | as | ion |
| --- | --- | --- | --- | --- |
| ten | de | ure | ti | ap |
| li | sign | gra | cuse | ence |
| ex | al | re | at | work |
| sci | note | ate | ply | dy |
| geb | at | tude | ra | sten |
| book | tion | tent | post | gram |
| home | his | tar | cess | ment |

1. _____
2. _____
3. _____
4. _____
5. _____
6. _____
7. _____
8. _____
9. _____
10. _____
11. _____
12. _____
13. _____
14. _____
15. _____
16. _____
17. _____

**Brain Aerobics** — Fractured Sports Terms

# FRACTURED SPORTS TERMS

There are 17 sports terms that have been broken up into two or three parts in the matrix below. Using each part only once, put the word parts together and write the sports terms on the lines below.

| tice | ner  | ble  | com  | vice |
|------|------|------|------|------|
| out  | tour | der  | bask | part |
| fair | tute | ee   | in   | time |
| pire | pen  | sti  | na   | drib |
| mer  | et   | ple  | for  | re   |
| ter  | ser  | quar | um   | tion |
| way  | prac | alty | ward | ment |
| sub  | fiel | ho   | fer  | back |

1. basket
2. completion
3. dribble
4. fairway
5. forward
6. homer
7. infielder
8. partner
9. penalty
10. practice
11. quarterback
12. referee
13. service
14. substitute
15. timeout
16. tournament
17. umpire

## Composing Palindromic Sentences

## Teacher's Guide

**About the Lesson:**

It isn't hard to think of palindromes with three letters. *Pop, pip, pup, pap,* and *pep* come easily to mind. For this lesson, your students are to do more than think of palindromes—they are to make up sentences composed only of palindromes. The examples given in the lesson should be enough to guide them, but if not, you might provide your students with another, such as "Did Dud eye Ada?" or "Did Hannah gag Lil?". If your students only use the palindromes offered in the lesson, their main problem will be a scarcity of verbs. Accordingly, they should try to come up with other palindromic verbs.

**Evaluating Student Responses:**

If your students abide by the rules of this word game, they will produce short sentences that have a subject, verb, and perhaps an object. When they have written their sentences, ask them to look at each sentence and identify the subject and predicate and also to see if they have punctuated the sentence properly. The sentence leading off the lesson begins with the interjection "Wow", and it has an exclamation mark. One or more of your students could start sentences with other interjections (*aha, heh, hah, oho*), and they should follow these words with exclamation marks.

Among the sentences that can be formed with only the palindromes listed in the lesson are these:

| | |
|---|---|
| Bob solos. | Ada did toot. |
| Mom sees Dad. | Mom (Nan, Lil, etc.) did peep. |
| Did Hanna gag Lil? | Sara's dad sees Otto (Bob, Dud, Ara, etc.). |
| Did Dud eye Ada? | Sara's mom sees Viv (Lil, Ava, Nan, etc.). |
| Dad sees Sara's tot. | Wow! Did Bob level Otto! |
| Did Sis peep? | Did Bob level Otto? |
| Oho! Did Bob pop Ara! | Mom sees Sara's kayak (tot, pullup, etc.). |

**Targeted Learner Outcomes:** The student will:

- learn the definition of a palindrome.

- write three or more sentences composed only of palindromes.

# EITHER WAY

Wow! Did Eve pop Bob!

Do you notice anything unusual about the sentence above? It contains only **palindromes**, words that can be read the same both forward and backward. The sentence itself isn't a palindrome, however. People have spent a lot of time trying to write sentences that can be read both from left to right and from right to left, though. One of the most famous sentences that can be read either way is: "Step on no pets."

Here are quite a few palindromes. Add as many as you can think of, especially any verbs.

| Asa | Dad | noon | Ada | | |
|---|---|---|---|---|---|
| pullup | dud | solos | tut | | |
| sees | Mom | radar | Abba | | |
| wow | mom | Mum | deed | | |
| did | Dad | mum | hah | | |
| Bob | dad | gig | pup | | |
| bob | pip | Hannah | level | | |
| Eve | gag | madam | huh | | |
| eve | toot | ma'am | so's | | |
| Pop | oho | eye | Sara's | | |
| pop | peep | stats | rotor | | |
| Ava | Sis | heh | sagas | | |
| bub | Nan | Lil | Viv | | |
| bib | tot | pep | tenet | | |
| pap | kayak | kook | ere | | |
| nun | eke | Otto | ewe | | |

Now write at least three complete sentences made up of combinations of palindromes. Your sentences must only contain palindromes, and they should be complete sentences with a subject and predicate, capital letter at the beginning, and proper punctuation. They can be as short as two words. You don't need to write the sentences so that they can be read backward. Just make sure all the words used are palindromes. For example, "Otto sees Anna." is a sentence with only palindromes.

1. _____
2. _____
3. _____
4. _____
5. _____

Brain Aerobics                                                                                      A Palindromic Portrait

Name: _____ Date: _____

# A PALINDROMIC PORTRAIT

Some given names and surnames are palindromes. These palindromic names can be the basis of an acrostic. Following are two examples:

**HANNAH**
Harried and nervous,
Anxious to please,
Never really completely at ease, but
Not a complainer;
Always tries her best—
Humble, conscientious girl.

**SELES**
Shining face and warm smile,
Excellent ground strokes,
Loses gracefully;
Energy is boundless—
Simply the best.

Choose from among these names and make one the basis for an acrostic. Your acrostic should give a good glimpse of the individual's personality.

Otto, Bob, Ada, Nan, Eve, Dud, Gig, Sis, Pop, Dad, Mom, Viv, Lil, Asa, Bub, Anna, Tippit, Reger, Omo, Reser, Dod, Reber, Sas, Lesel, Karak

|   |   |
|---|---|
|   |   |
|   |   |
|   |   |
|   |   |
|   |   |
|   |   |

Whether you chose a real person or an imaginary person for your acrostic, you now have the basis for a character sketch. A character sketch is making a portrait of someone in words. The objective is to present the person so that the readers get a good idea of what he or she is like. Readers should be able to learn enough that they feel they have met the subject and almost know that person. The appearance, traits, idiosyncrasies, and accomplishments of the subject provide the fabric of the character sketch.

Write a first draft of your character sketch on your own paper and then go over it, looking for mistakes in organization, grammar, punctuation, and spelling. Then rewrite your sketch and have a classmate read it. Finally, taking into consideration your classmate's comments, write a final draft.

Brain Aerobics                                                                                              Find the Word

# FIND THE WORD

*Finding Hidden Words in Grids*

## Teacher's Guide

**About the Lesson:**

"Find the Word" is analogous to the familar "find the hidden figure" picture puzzle, but it is more difficult. It forces students to scan the letters in ways that are different from the conventional left-to-right eye movement. Most students will scrutinize the letters for quite a while before a word can be made out. Give them enough time to link up the letters. If they don't solve the first puzzle, tell them to tackle the next one and then go back to it later.

**Evaluating Student Responses:**

These are the hidden words in the three matrices:

1. The word is pretender.

| O | S | (E) | (T) |
|---|---|---|---|
| F | (P) | (R) | (E) |
| H | I | G | (N) |
| A | (R) | (E) | (D) |

2. The word is octagonal.

| R | (O) | (A) | (G) |
|---|---|---|---|
| E | (C) | (T) | (O) |
| P | I | (A) | (N) |
| M | J | (L) | U |

3. The word is succulent.

| (S) | (U) | P | R |
|---|---|---|---|
| E | (C) | (C) | I |
| (T) | B | (U) | S |
| (N) | (E) | (L) | O |

**Targeted Learner Outcomes:** The student will:

- solve three puzzles.

- devise a hidden word puzzle that can be presented to classmates.

Brain Aerobics — Find the Word

# FIND THE WORD

| R | O | B | E |
|---|---|---|---|
| P | S | T | A |
| L | U | G | U |
| C | F | I | T |

There is a nine-letter word in the grid above. The letters of the word are sequentially arranged horizontally and vertically, but not diagonally, in contiguous squares. Each letter is only used once. The hidden word is an adjective meaning "very lovely." Can you make out the word?

What is it? _____

To show you how to work the puzzle, we have circled the letters of the mystery word below.

| R | O | (B) | (E) |
|---|---|---|---|
| P | S | T | (A) |
| (L) | (U) | G | (U) |
| C | (F) | (I) | (T) |

Now try finding the hidden words in the three grids below. Circle the letters of each word.

1. The word means "someone who makes believe." _____

| O | S | E | T |
|---|---|---|---|
| F | P | R | E |
| H | I | G | N |
| A | R | E | D |

Brain Aerobics  Find the Word

Name: _____  Date: _____

# FIND THE WORD (cont.)

2. The word means "having eight sides." _____

| R | O | A | G |
|---|---|---|---|
| E | C | T | O |
| P | I | A | N |
| M | J | L | U |

3. The word means "full of juice." _____

| S | U | P | R |
|---|---|---|---|
| A | C | C | I |
| T | B | U | S |
| N | E | L | O |

4. Try to make up your own hidden word puzzle. Once you have the puzzle and solution figured out, make a copy on your own paper and exchange with a classmate.

   Clue: _____

   Answer: _____

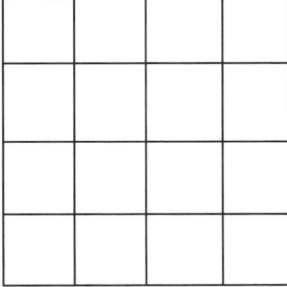

Brain Aerobics                                                                                           Animals in Hiding

# ANIMALS IN HIDING

*Finding the Names of Animals in Words*

## Teacher's Guide

**About the Lesson:**

As hinted in the lesson, students who are skilled in playing anagrams will sail through most of the lesson easily. They may be challenged, however, when they read the end because at that point they will have to create their own "beastly" words. For the first two parts of the lesson, your students will ferret out the names of animals by putting together letters that make up the names. Spelling words correctly is the skill that is brought out in this lesson.

**Evaluating Student Responses:**

Following are answers for the first set of prompts. We may have missed a few animals, so this may not be a complete listing. Occasionally there is a little humor in a response, such as the *slug* in *goulash*.

1. pony
2. bird
3. horse
4. lynx
5. hen
6. crow, cow
7. mice
8. owl, wolf, fowl
9. fox
10. frog
11. spider
12. ant
13. asp
14. rat
15. slug
16. hog
17. parrot
18. swan
19. wren, tern
20. tiger

Animals hiding in other animals.

1. cow
2. calf
3. ant, rat
4. gorilla
5. pig
6. eel, ant

Answers will vary, but among the words that have two animals hiding in them are the following:

1. kaleidoscope: kid and asp
2. sheepherder: sheep and deer
3. bureaucrat: bear, cat, and rat
4. feelingly: fly and eel
5. implacable: camel and impala

**Targeted Learner Outcomes:** The student will:

- find the name of animals in two sets of prompts.

- come up with at least five words that contain the letters of at least two animal names.

Brain Aerobics | Animals in Hiding

Name: _____ Date: _____

# ANIMALS IN HIDING

You can surely see the *cat* in *catsup*, but can you see the *hare* in *shear*? If you've played anagrams a lot, you won't have any trouble finding the other animals hiding in these words. Write the name of the animal hidden inside the word on each line. Some words may have more than one hidden animal. You only need to find one animal for each word.

1. phony _____
2. bridle _____
3. shore _____
4. larynx _____
5. heathen _____
6. coward _____
7. chime _____
8. fellow _____
9. exfoliate _____
10. forget _____
11. striped _____
12. fantasy _____
13. praise _____
14. crystal _____
15. goulash _____
16. ghost _____
17. rapport _____
18. answer _____
19. winter _____
20. goiter _____

What animals are hiding in these other animals?

1. crow _____
2. falcon _____
3. panther _____
4. alligator _____
5. pigeon _____
6. elephant _____

Can you think of any words where two animals are hiding? For example, there are a *bee* and a *moth* in *behemoth*. See if you can come up with at least five words that have at least two words hidden in them. Remember, insects are animals.

1. _____
2. _____
3. _____
4. _____
5. _____
6. _____

# ANSWER KEYS

**Gloryjumpers and Spoilworms (p. 9)**
Original compound words:
1. spoilsport
2. bookworm
3. glad-hander
4. scatterbrain
5. puddlejumper
6. blabbermouth
7. nitpicker
8. doomsayer
9. guttersnipe
10. gloryhound
11. jitterbug
12. rugrat

**The Rhyming Game (p. 11)**
1. hot tot
2. glum chum
3. big pig
4. great mate
5. coy boy or shy guy
6. bad fad
7. smart start
8. rare pair
9. tough stuff
10. top cop
11. fake snake
12. bear's lair
13. cook book
14. slow foe

**The Rhyming Game #2 (p. 12)**
1. funny bunny
2. stricken chicken
3. puffy toughie
4. yellow fellow
5. handy Andy
6. funny money
7. slender vendor
8. heady Teddy
9. frantic antic
10. hefty lefty
11. very hairy
12. starvin' Marvin

**Triangles (p. 13)**
1. "O to win once!"
2. I do dig boys."
3. "I am too cold."

**More Triangles (p. 14–15)**
1. "O my bad head!"
2. a "no" was okay.
3. "O to hit hard!"
4. "I am not here."

**Three-Way Triangles (p. 16–17)**
1.

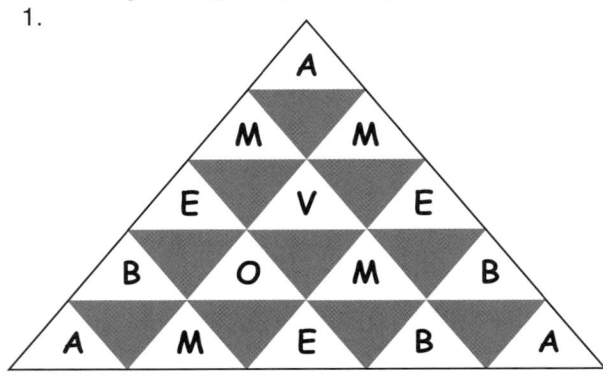

2.

3.
(or AVA)

**Find the Twisted Word (p. 22)**

1. EXPLAIN
2. READING
3. PROJECT
4. FIGURES

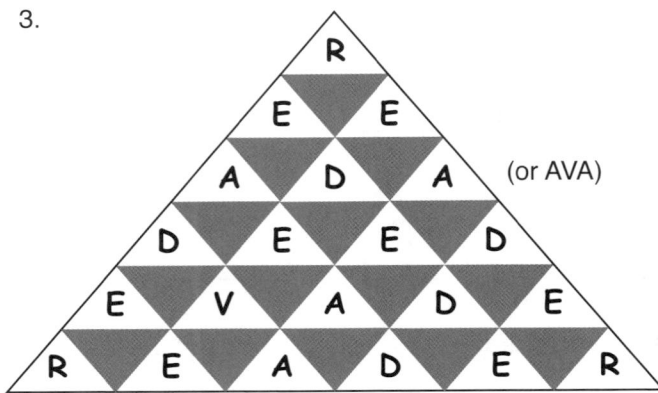

## More Twisted and Hidden Words (p. 23)

1. CAPITAL

| P | S | I | T |
|---|---|---|---|
| K | A | P | A |
| Z | C | N | L |
| B | U | Y | O |

2. DEPICTS

| R | O | Z | K |
|---|---|---|---|
| B | S | K | M |
| C | T | L | U |
| I | P | E | D |

3. WRITING

| Y | L | O | P |
|---|---|---|---|
| E | W | S | G |
| A | R | I | N |
| M | U | T | I |

4. PERIOD

| A | S | E | P |
|---|---|---|---|
| N | I | R | K |
| F | O | Q | B |
| S | D | C | U |

## Magic Squares (p. 24–25)

1.
| U | R | G | E |
|---|---|---|---|
| R | O | O | M |
| G | O | B | I |
| E | M | I | T |

2.
| T | A | L | E |
|---|---|---|---|
| A | V | I | D |
| L | I | T | E |
| E | D | E | N |

3.
| P | I | C | S |
|---|---|---|---|
| I | D | E | A |
| C | E | N | T |
| S | A | T | E |

## More (and Harder) Magic Squares (p. 26)

1.
| S | E | N | S | E |
|---|---|---|---|---|
| E | D | E | M | A |
| N | E | V | E | R |
| S | M | E | L | L |
| E | A | R | L | Y |

2.
| S | P | E | A | K |
|---|---|---|---|---|
| P | E | A | C | E |
| E | A | T | E | R |
| A | C | E | R | B |
| K | E | R | B | S |

## Mr. Reynolds' Maze (p. 28)

To decode the message that Mr. Reynolds gave to his children, change each letter to the one two spaces to the left in the alphabet (c = a, d = b, e = c, etc.).

The letter "e" is the one that occurs most frequently in English.

The message was: "When there is a choice go to the left."

Walter's message would be: "Let me out of here!"

This is the path through the maze that is quickest:

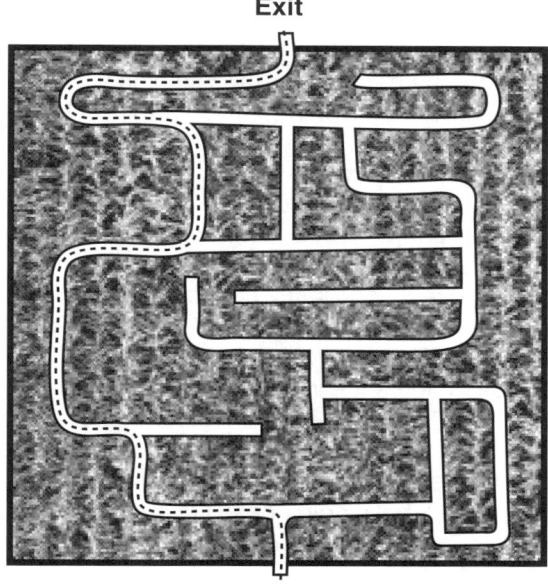

## Can You Reverse Them? (p. 33)

These are possible interpretations of the 14 reversed sayings. Students should choose at least five sentences that they think make sense when reversed.
1. May all your troubles be small ones.
   Reversal: May all your small ones be trouble.
   Heavens no! We wouldn't want that benediction.
2. Where there's a will, there's a way.
   Reversal: Where there's a way, there's a will.
   Yes. This would indicate that someone showed the way.

3. Time waits for no one.
   Reversal: No one waits for time.
   Couldn't be more untrue. Everyone does a lot of waiting.
4. Nobody loves a loser.
   Reversal: A loser loves nobody.
   Yes. That is possible.
5. It's better to be safe than sorry.
   Reversal: It's better to be sorry than safe.
   No. This doesn't work.
6. Don't count your chickens before they're hatched.
   Reversal: Don't hatch your chickens before they're counted.
   Yes. This makes sense if you want a certain number of chicks to be hatched.
7. Beggars can't be choosers.
   Reversal: Choosers can't be beggars.
   Maybe. If you could choose, you wouldn't want to be a beggar.
8. A penny saved is a penny earned.
   Reversal: A penny earned is a penny saved.
   No. We usually don't save all our pennies.
9. The bigger they are, the harder they fall.
   Reversal: The harder they fall, the bigger they are.
   Yes, if the amount of weight determines how hard they fall.
10. Still waters run deep.
    Reversal: Deep waters run still.
    Yes. It's about the same thing.
11. He laughs best who laughs last.
    Reversal: He laughs last who laughs best.
    Yes. It's the same notion; the syntax is just altered.
12. If the shoe fits, wear it.
    Reversal: If the shoe wears, fit it.
    Yes, if "fit it" means adjust or repair it after the shoe has worn.
13. All that glitters isn't gold.
    Reversal: All that's gold doesn't glitter.
    Yes. A lot of gold things don't glitter (aren't ostentatious or obvious).
14. Many hands make light work.
    Reversal: Light hands make many work.
    Yes. Many (individuals) have to work when light (lazy) hands are applied to the task.

**Fractured School Words (p. 34)**
(Words may be written in any order.)
1. algebra        2. apply         3. assignment
4. attention      5. attitude      6. detention
7. excuse         8. grammar       9. graduate
10. history       11. homework     12. listen
13. notebook      14. posture      15. recess
16. science       17. tardy

**Fractured Sports Words (p. 35)**
(Words may be written in any order.)
1. basket         2. dribble       3. completion
4. fairway        5. forward       6. homer
7. infielder      8. partner       9. penalty
10. practice      11. quarterback  12. referee
13. service       14. substitute   15. timeout
16. tournament    17. umpire